"Before there were any Indians, the To-whon-an-ung-wa lived in that place. There were many of them. They were of many kinds—birds, animals, lizards, and such things—but they looked like people. . . . For some reason the people in that place were bad. Because they were bad Shin-awav, Coyote, turned them all into rocks; some standing in rows, some sitting down, some holding on to others. You can see their faces, with paint on them just as they were before they became rocks. The name of that place is Angka-ku-wass-a-wits."

Story told in 1936 by
Indian Dick, an aged Piute
living on the Kaibab
Reservation.

"There are thousands of red, white, purple, and vermilion colored rocks, of all sizes, resembling sentinels on the walls of castles, monks and priests in their robes, attendants, cathedrals and congregations. There are deep caverns and rooms resembling ruins of prisons, castles, churches with their guarded walls, battlements, spires, and steeples, niches and recesses, presenting the wildest and most wonderful scene that the eye of man ever beheld, in fact it is one of the wonders of the world."

T. C. Bailey, 1876
U.S. Deputy Surveyor

"The glory of all this rock work is seen in the
Pink Cliffs.... The resemblances to strict
architectural forms are often startling. The upper
tier of the vast amphitheater is one mighty
colonnade. Standing obelisks, prostrate columns,
shattered capitals, panels, niches, buttresses,
repetitions of symmetrical forms, all bring vividly
before the mind suggestions of the work of giant
hands, a race of genii once rearing temples of
rock, but now chained up in a spell of
enchantment, while their structures are falling in
ruins through centuries of decay."

Clarence E. Dutton, 1880
Captain of Ordnance,
U.S.A.

"From the bottoms of the alcoves cut into the Pink Cliffs rise spires and ridges, and many of them are filled to the brim with literally hundreds of towers, needles, cathedrals, narrow mesas, and myriads of fantastic figures that stand alone or are grouped about buttresses of the enclosing walls, which themselves are decorated with windows and niches of many shapes. Every erosional feature possible to make in rocks of this kind seems to be represented by innumerable examples."

Herbert E. Gregory, 1951
United States Geological
Survey

BRYCE CANYON
NATIONAL PARK

Photography and text by Fred Hirschmann

Bryce Canyon Natural History Association
Bryce Canyon National Park, Utah 84764

Contents

Uncaptioned Photos

Cover: Thor's Hammer basking in reflected light of sunrise.

First frontispiece: The Pink Cliffs at Agua Canyon.

Second frontispiece with Indian Dick quote: Bryce amphitheater viewed from Inspiration Point.

Third frontispiece with T.C. Bailey quote: Natural Bridge with early winter snow.

Fourth frontispiece with Clarence E. Dutton quote: Sun rising behind Thor's Hammer

Fifth frontispiece with Herbert E. Gregory quote: Richly colored hoodoos of Agua Canyon.

Sixth frontispiece: Autumn color of bigtooth maples near Lower Podunk Creek.

Title page: The Silent City.

Back cover: Thousands of tiny ice prisms creating sundogs around the rising sun.

Library of Congress Catalog Card Number: 88-70555

ISBN 0-929054-01-6—Softcover Edition
ISBN 0-929054-00-8—Hardcover Edition

Copyright, photography, text and illustrations: Fred Hirschmann

Designer: Fred Hirschmann, Nature's Design Press

Editor: Eugenia M. Horstman

National Park Service Consultant: Margaret Littlejohn

Typographer: Prepress Graphics, Flagstaff, Arizona

Printer: Dai Nippon Printing Company, Ltd., Tokyo, Japan

Publisher: Bryce Canyon Natural History Association
        Bryce Canyon National Park, Utah 84764

Fourth Printing

Discovering Bryce Canyon

My first look at the limestone pinnacles, obelisks, towers, and castles of Bryce Canyon occurred nearly a decade ago. My seasonal ranger job in Yellowstone ended in early November. I loaded all my worldly possessions in the back of a 1958 Chevy pickup purchased for $250 and headed south. I was unemployed and had no real destination in mind except to explore the canyon country of southern Utah until my meager savings disappeared.

I arrived at Bryce Canyon about 10 p.m. and found both campgrounds snowed shut. A small sign indicated camping was permissible in the plowed

Sun, drifted snow, and lone hoodoo.

Visitor Center parking lot. It had snowed all the way south from Yellowstone, and here at Bryce Canyon the storm was finally breaking. Ragged shreds of clouds raced over the edge of the Paunsaugunt Plateau. Thousands of tiny ice prisms were wafted along by a sharp northwest wind. The moon was nearly full and illuminated ghostly ponderosa pines bearing heavy loads of fresh snow. I strapped on wooden crosscountry skis and headed for the Bryce rim.

That first look over the edge and down among the legions of limestone spires gripped me with awe and fascination. The interplay of racing moon shadows, sparkling ice crystals, and hundreds of snow-draped hoodoos was magical. The moonlight gave Bryce Canyon depth. The shadows enveloped mysterious scenery that awaited the light of day for in-depth exploration. As the cold snow protested every kick of my skis with a loud squeak, I thought to myself, "Boy,

would I love spending a winter at Bryce Canyon."

Eventually the piercing cold overcame my yearning to see more of the canyon, and I skied back among the pines to the warmth of a down sleeping bag.

With the break of day, I melted ice that had accumulated overnight on my mustache and hair. Then I entered the park Visitor Center and had a friendly chat with LaKay Quilter from Henrieville, Utah. I inquired whether the park might be hiring anyone for the winter. LaKay replied that the previous day the staff was trying desperately to hire someone, but had failed. I asked if I could talk with the person doing the hiring. LaKay fetched the park's Resource Management Specialist.

Jim Hannah, a big friendly ranger, told me a tale of woe concerning a surprise governmentwide hiring freeze that had been initiated the previous day. The park wished to hire a person with plenty of winter experience. Duties included breaking the under-the-rim trails after each storm so snowshoeing visitors wouldn't become lost, taking daily air quality readings to monitor pollutants from the region's coal-fired power plants, periodically checking the parking lots at overlooks to make sure visitors hadn't carbon monoxided themselves in tightly closed cars, and shoveling snow. Jim said if I had come to the park yesterday, I could have had the job. I then explained I *was* in the park the prior day. I had arrived about 10 p.m., skied to the rim, and then camped overnight in the parking lot. Jim asked,

Fog lifting from formations along the Navajo Trail.

"Are you sure you were here yesterday?" I replied, "Yes, my ski tracks are out there to prove it." Jim smiled and disappeared to talk with the Administrative Officer. The two men returned and gave me a stack of papers to sign. I guess the moonlight ski to the rim was my official park orientation tour.

The winter working at Bryce Canyon was incredible. Snowstorm after snowstorm blanketed Utah's high plateaus. At first, the old-timers of Tropic, Cannonville, and Henrieville claimed the winter of 1936–37 was worse. Subsequent snowfall silenced their stories. I was happily plodding along on snowshoes and skis absorbing the winter beauty. It is a tough life, but somebody has to accept these remote government jobs at national parks in the dead of winter. Actually, the quiet time from November to April allows a rejuvenation of spirit. Summer will come accompanied by hoards of park visitors. With the onslaught of crowds comes park ranger nightmares of waking up from an intense dream of telling the thousandth person in a row, "Ma'am, the bathrooms are out the door and to the left."

January 25, 1979, brought an overnight snowfall of 25 inches on top of the four feet of snow already blanketing the ground. At 8:30 the next morning, disaster struck the Syrett family who had kept the beautiful stone fireplace of Ruby's Inn dancing with flames for 54 winters. The previous summer the family had constructed a 38- by 60-foot banquet hall. After the snowstorm abated, Bob Syrett stuck his head into the room and saw that a truss had snapped and was projecting through the ceiling. The Syrett brothers grabbed shovels and were crossing from an adjacent roof when they heard timbers crack followed by a muffled woof. Immediately before them, the roof collapsed.

Bob Syrett later bemused, "We were really fortunate it went in the morning. That night a banquet had been scheduled for the local Lions Club. The injuries and loss of life would have been terrible had it gone then."

The collapse of the roof at Ruby's Inn just north of the park spurred Bryce Canyon's staff into a midwinter frenzy of snow removal. Everyone from the Assistant Superintendent to the lowest one on the totem pole, who happened to be me, was up on the park roofs shoveling snow. Before the snow could be removed, nails popped through walls, joists cracked with loud reports, and doors jammed shut. Luckily, no more structures were lost.

With the spring melt, funding for my job drained away. I left Bryce Canyon in May but have returned to the land of hoodoos every year since to explore and photograph the park through the seasons.

What a pleasure to intimately experience Bryce

Skier telemarking beneath the Bryce Canyon rim.

Canyon through one of the severest winters on record. The cold and moisture wrought upon Bryce Canyon by the Paunsaugunt Plateau's elevation of 7,600 to 9,200 feet above sea level is vital in shaping the geology of the park and determining the zones of plant and animal life.

The most important agent of erosion at Bryce Canyon is the simple freezing and thawing of water. During a typical year, close to 200 days occur where the daytime temperature rises above 32°F yet the overnight low falls below freezing. Ice crystals lift tiny bits of rock perpendicularly from a slope, and subsequent melting vertically drops the debris slightly downslope. Day after day, the freeze-thaw cycle causes a nearly indiscernible downslope creep of material.

Considerably more dramatic sculpting comes from the expansion of water as it freezes within vertical cracks that run through the Claron Formation. Ice wedges topple huge portions of the limestone spires called hoodoos. If you are skeptical of road signs saying "watch for falling rock" because you have never seen a rock fall, just grab a hard hat and take a walk below the Bryce Canyon rim during spring thaw. You will witness erosion in action as rocks tumble all over the place. During the past few decades, many landmarks beneath the rim have changed. Nearly two-thirds of the Sentinel sheared away in 1986. The camel's head fell off the Camel and the Wiseman in 1977, and the arch in Oastler's Castle collapsed in 1964.

The crack of thunder in July and August marks the season of gully-washing downpours that carry debris away from the park toward the Paria River. Freeze-and-thaw action coupled with

White-tailed prairie dog at burrow.

Mule deer browsing.

Margaret Littlejohn

water transport during periods of heavy rain causes the Paunsaugunt Plateau rim to retreat westward at an average rate of approximately 1½ feet per century. Old hoodoos topple, but new legions emerge from the retreating escarpment. In spite of the rapid erosion, Bryce Canyon will maintain its general appearance for centuries to come.

The soft rock in which Bryce's intricate beauty is incised is some of the youngest on the Colorado Plateau. Thirty-three million to 53 million years ago, much of what is now central and southwestern Utah was covered by silty, low-lying lakes. In the vicinity of Bryce Canyon at least 500 to 800 feet of limestone, siltstone, sandstone, and dolomite accumulated. Geologists usually refer to the rocks comprising Utah's Pink Cliffs as the Claron Formation, although the names Wasatch Formation and Cedar Breaks Formation can be found in Print. Beneath the Claron Formation rest rock layers that are exposed in Zion National Park, and deeper yet are likely those found in the Grand Canyon.

Tremendous regional uplifting began approximately 15 million years ago. West of the park, the Sevier Fault is quite discernible at the mouth of Red Canyon where black basalt abuts red Claron limestone. And to the east of the park, uplifting has raised the Table Cliffs at the southernmost extent of the Aquarius Plateau 2,000 feet above the identical formation in Bryce Canyon. During millions of years following the uplifting, the Paria River carved a large amphitheater into the faulted blocks of the Paunsaugunt and Aquarius plateaus. The intricate beauty of Bryce Canyon is the Paria River's handiwork.

Myriad erosional forms eloquently speak of Bryce Canyon's harsh climate tearing into the backbone of the Paunsaugunt Plateau. This same harsh climate is the source of moisture and coolness that sprinkle and spread the mantle of green life across Bryce Canyon National Park. Below the plateau rim in the lowest areas of the park near the town of Tropic, a forest of Utah juniper and pinyon pine survives where a scant 12 inches of precipitation fall annually. Precipitation increases with gain in elevation. On top of the plateau in the northern half of the park 14 to 16 inches of annual moisture nurture stately ponderosa pines. The Paunsaugunt Plateau gradually rises to the south. Dense stands of white fir and Douglas fir of the Canadian life zone replace the open ponderosa pine forest in the highest elevations of the park. Near Rainbow Point, some years may bring more than 25 inches of precipitation including more than 200 inches of snow!

Nearly barren limestone ridges exposed to the harshest of elements support ancient, gnarled and scarred bristlecone pines. The oldest bristlecone in the park has witnessed the sun rising over Canaan Peak for about 1,700 years.

Wildlife abounds on the protected lands of the park. Mule deer frequent meadows and forested regions. From March through October,

Steller's jay in ponderosa pine.

hustle and bustle occurs in the prairie dog towns of open meadows. Threatened white-tailed prairie dogs raise their young and acquire healthy supplies of fat prior to winter hibernation. Golden-mantled ground squirrels and chipmunks are abundant along the plateau rim. Predators include coyotes, foxes, bobcats, great horned owls, golden eagles, and considerably rarer peregrine falcons and mountain lions.

Bryce Canyon is a land of incredible scenery. The photographs that follow capture only part of the beauty. Missing is the sweet aroma of ponderosa pine on spring and summer days, the chattering of a tree squirrel who interrupted a session of gathering cones from a Douglas fir to scold your presence, and the sound of wind rushing past hoodoos and through pine boughs. When visiting Bryce Canyon, by all means, park your automobile and walk the trails. Rise with the sun and watch the warm orange light radiate across the hoodoos. Hike to the bottom of the canyon and absorb the impressive grandeur of the Pink Cliffs. Fill your lungs with the clean air of Utah's high plateaus. Let your eyes feast on the broad expanse of thousands of square miles of undeveloped, wild western scenery.

Also, consider visiting Bryce Canyon when the hoodoos are blanketed in winter's white wraps. Perhaps you will ski to the rim of the Paunsaugunt Plateau beneath the light of the full moon and watch thousands of tiny ice prisms sparkle in the frigid air.

Bryce Canyon's scenery is likely to enthrall you to the point of returning again and again to gaze at nature's finest erosional handiwork.

Right: Formations below Bryce Point with melting snow of early spring.

A limber pine growing on Sunset Point frames Boat Mesa beyond the Bryce Amphitheater. The top of Boat Mesa is protected by erosion-resistant conglomerate deposited above the softer Claron Formation.

The Queen's Garden is a magical place of ponderosa pines and Douglas firs scattered among pink and orange hoodoos. A popular hiking trail descends 320 feet from Sunrise Point into the heart of the Queen's Garden.

A natural window in the Claron Formation provides a fine
view of the Chinese Wall south of Campbell Canyon. East-
west-running ridge crest walls are common below the rim in
the northern portion of the park. A cap of harder dolomitic
limestone temporarily protects the walls from ravages of
erosion.

The retreating edge of the Paunsaugunt Plateau between
Sunrise Point and Sunset Point is so steep that few plants can
gain a foothold. When slopes become greater than 45 degrees,
hoodoos seldom form.

Appropriately named, Fairyland Canyon holds myriad
fanciful erosional forms. These hoodoos glow with golden
hues in the rich light of morning.

At 5 a.m. during the summer most Bryce Canyon visitors
remain tucked beneath their covers. Facing east, the
escarpment of the Paunsaugunt Plateau is painted with pastel
colors during dawn.

Washes draining toward the Paria River from Bryce Canyon transport tremendous loads of sediment during spring melting of snow and after heavy summer rains. Light-colored gravel, derived almost entirely from Claron Formation limestone and dolomite, carpets the floor of Fairyland Canyon Wash. Occasional pebbles of black basalt likely came from volcanic activity occurring north of what is now the park 19 to 37 million years ago.

The narrow spire of The Sentinel stands among the hoodoos below Sunset Point. Rapid erosion of Bryce Canyon is often dramatic. Fully two-thirds of The Sentinel sheared away in the early summer of 1986.

The Pink Cliffs near Yovimpa Point bask in the crisp orange light of sunset. Beyond is uninhabited country with place names like No Man's Mesa, Lower Death Valley, and The Cockscomb. The clear views and quiet solitude of Yovimpa Point may not last forever. Plans keep resurfacing to strip-mine coal a mere three miles south of the park border.

Across The Promontory from Yovimpa Point is 9,105-foot Rainbow Point. A hoodoo affectionately called The Poodle sits just below the Paunsaugunt Plateau Rim.

Smoke from forest fires in California provides a hazy
backdrop for a hoodoo named The Hunter. Iron oxides
impart vivid orange and red colors to the Claron Formation
at Agua Canyon.

Ravens find Bryce Canyon a special place. Scores of the large
black birds spend each night roosting among limestone spires
in the Silent City. Raindrops glisten on a raven feather
resting on the canyon floor.

Hoodoos are defined as "pinnacles, pillars, or odd-shaped rocks left standing by the forces of erosion." Some of the tallest hoodoos in the park, towering 200 feet, form the Silent City between Inspiration Point and Sunset Point.

Once a hoodoo emerges from a retreating slope, the vertical surface of the spire tends to shed moisture. The weathering actions of freezing and thawing water diminish. These hoodoos in Fairyland Canyon disintegrate more slowly than the rolling badlands on which they rest.

The first light of sunrise strikes the rim of the Bryce
Amphitheater near Inspiration Point. Within minutes pastel
colors of dawn fade, and fiery orange illuminates hundreds
of hoodoos.

A tiny plant struggles for existence among limestone talus.
Conditions for life are severe on the breaks of the
Paunsaugunt Plateau. Steep gravel slopes rapidly shed
moisture. Mammoth hoodoos block light from the sun.
Desiccating winds sap what little water exists.

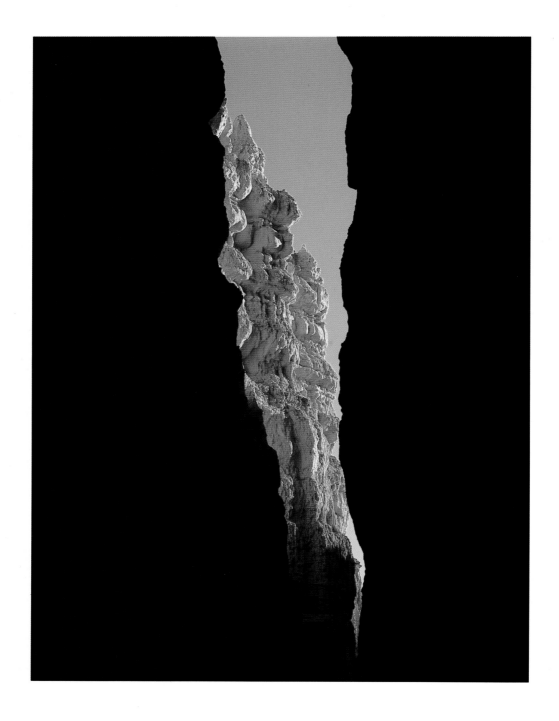

Wall Street, within The Silent City, is a dark and mysterious place. The canyon walls climb approximately 200 feet, yet are only 20 feet apart. The sky becomes a narrow blue strip when viewed from below.

From Inspiration Point, The Silent City looks like an impenetrable fortress of hoodoos. Vertical cracks, known by geologists as joints, often control the location of hoodoos. Here, legions of spires stand in orderly rows.

Fifteen miles across the Paria Amphitheater, Table Cliff Plateau rises 2,000 feet higher than identical rock formations in the northern part of Bryce Canyon. Beginning about 16 million years ago, uplifting split what is now southern Utah into seven high plateaus. Table Cliff Plateau is the southernmost extension of the Aquarius Plateau.

Rapid downcutting by the Paria River has obliterated much evidence of the Paunsaugunt Fault that lifted the Aquarius Plateau high above the Paunsaugunt Plateau. Headwaters of the Paria River have sliced deeply into the soft Claron Formation and sculpted the fantastic scenery of Bryce Canyon.

Ninety percent of Bryce Canyon's 60 miles of hiking trails is below the Paunsaugunt Plateau rim. Hikers exploring the Queen's Garden pass a large white hoodoo lacking the salmon-colored stain of iron oxide.

Hoodoos in the Queen's Garden rise above twisted skeletons of ponderosa pines. As the old veterans slowly decompose, young ponderosa pines and patches of greenleaf manzanita gain a precious hold on life.

Agua Canyon at sunrise is one of the most beautiful sights in
the park. A green mantle of limber pine, Douglas fir, white
fir, and blue spruce surrounds the brilliant orange hoodoos.

A Douglas fir and limber pine struggle to survive among the
hoodoos and badlands of the Queen's Garden. Lower
elevations in the northern part of the park produce a drier
climate. Trees become widely spaced, reducing competition
for scarce resources.

Clusters of hoodoos rise from ridges within the Bryce
Amphitheater. Ancient lake sediments of the Claron
Formation erode into hundreds of intricate forms whose
shapes and designs are wilder than a child's imagination.

Bryce Canyon is a land of living geology. Hoodoos disintegrate, and the escarpment of the Paunsaugunt Plateau
retreats westward. Along the Navajo Trail two boulders that
tumbled off nearby spires offer mute testimony to the ever-
present forces of erosion.

Rapid retreat of the Paunsaugunt Plateau rim exposes the roots of a fairly young limber pine near Sunrise Point. On the average, the rim is eroding at a rate of 1½ feet per century. Coring of annual growth rings on exposed trees helps geologists measure the loss of sediment.

The Paria River, a tributary of the Colorado, dives into soft Navajo Sandstone east of the park. Before Squaw Creek empties into the Paria, sediment derived from The Promontory between Rainbow Point and Yovimpa Point helped carve an exquisite slot canyon 125 feet deep, yet only a few feet wide.

A new day begins as the sun peeks around the Table Cliff Plateau. Thor's Hammer, The Pope, and hundreds of unnamed hoodoos will soon bask in the warmth of morning light.

Between the fading of stars and the rising of the sun, magic colors of dawn paint The Silent City viewed from Sunset Point. The full moon sets as the sun clears the eastern horizon.

Dusk envelops hoodoos along the Peekaboo Trail. Evening is usually a time of peace and stillness at Bryce Canyon.

Facing east, the Bryce Canyon escarpment catches sunset light only on the highest exposed ridges and hoodoos. The Claron Formation east of Bryce Point contrasts with duller colored sandstone and shales beyond park borders.

Fresh snow accents the Sinking Ship, Table Cliff Plateau, and
Bristlecone Point as evening arrives over the Bryce
Amphitheater. Tension near the Paunsaugunt Fault tilted
normally flat-lying beds of the Claron Formation at the
Sinking Ship and to a lesser extent on Bristlecone Point.

Chemical weathering removes weak cement of calcium
carbonate that binds Claron Limestone. Grottoes, like these
below Sunrise Point, often form in vertical walls.

Gambel oak forms thickets in protected areas such as Water Canyon. Autumn frosts have started turning this Gambel oak golden-brown.

Thor's Hammer and The Sentinel are dwarfed by the slope of the Paunsaugunt Plateau below Sunset Point. The Bryce Amphitheater contains some of the tallest and best developed hoodoos in the world.

Seepage near Riggs Spring supports a meadow of shoulder-high rubber rabbitbrush. A California sister butterfly feeds on nectar from the blossoms.

Found only on limestone slopes in Bryce Canyon National Park and nearby Red Canyon, Reveal paintbrush is an endangered plant endemic to the Paunsaugunt Plateau. In addition to making sugars through photosynthesis, Reveal paintbrush parasitizes the roots of nearby plants to gain nourishment.

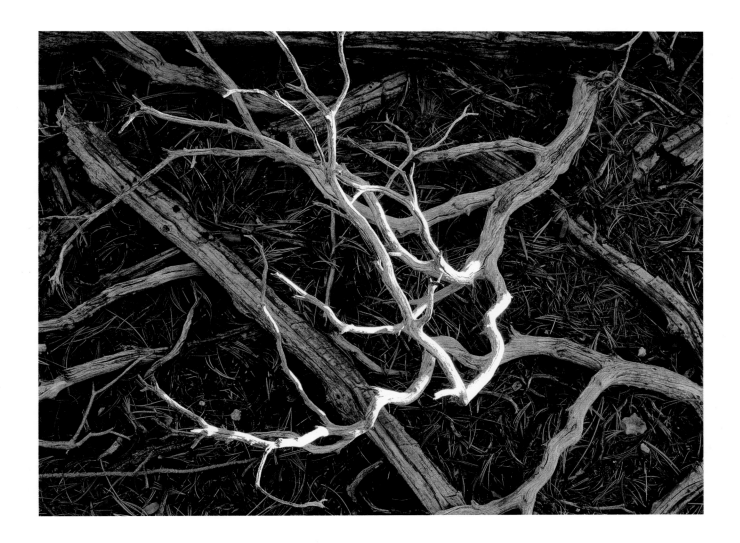

As dignified in death as it was in life, a weather-sculpted snag graces a limestone ridge below Bryce Point. Dry air and temperatures that remain below freezing during much of the year retard the rotting of wood.

Deadwood from greenleaf manzanita, limber pine, and ponderosa pine covers the forest floor on top of the Paunsaugunt Plateau near Agua Canyon. The open forests common to the northern half of Bryce Canyon National Park are replaced by dense stands of spruce, fir, and pine at the higher elevations found in the southern half of the park.

An early spring bloomer, greenleaf manzanita splashes pink blossoms across Bryce Canyon in April and May. Later in the summer, the fruits resemble tiny apples. *Manzanita* is Spanish for "little apple."

Greenleaf manzanita blankets a portion of The Promontory beyond Yovimpa Point. The leathery leaves remain green all winter. Their upright position reduces desiccation from wind and searing summer heat on the surface of rocky slopes.

Ponderosa pines, bigtooth maples, and yucca growing in
Corral Hollow frame a view of the Pink Cliffs near Yovimpa
Point. Beneath the Bryce rim, plants associated with the
desert meet the montane forests of Utah's high plateaus.

Autumn leaves of water birch decorate a small waterfall in
Jolley Hollow. A handful of perennially flowing springs occurs
beneath the rim. Running surface water is rare in Bryce
Canyon.

From the dark recesses of Wall Street, a Douglas fir has grown tall to place its canopy in direct sunlight. Two park visitors marvel at the tenacity for life exhibited by this healthy tree during its first 700 years.

One word sums up conditions for life on the breaks of Bryce Canyon—harsh. Natural stucco washing off nearby hoodoos plasters older leaves of ground-hugging Oregon grape. The plant continues photosynthesizing through new sprigs of green growth.

On well-drained limestone ridges exposed to the most desiccating winds, bristlecone pines maintain a tenacious hold on life. Where other species of trees fail to survive, bristlecones ever so slowly raise their weatherbeaten forms to the sky. The Bristlecone Loop Trail near Rainbow Point meanders through a grove of these stately veterans.

Through the centuries that bristlecones live, the Bryce landscape changes. Erosion strips away the limestone soils that nurtured the tree's roots centuries ago. In the face of severe winds, a bristlecone pine topples. Hundreds of years will pass before the deadwood disappears.

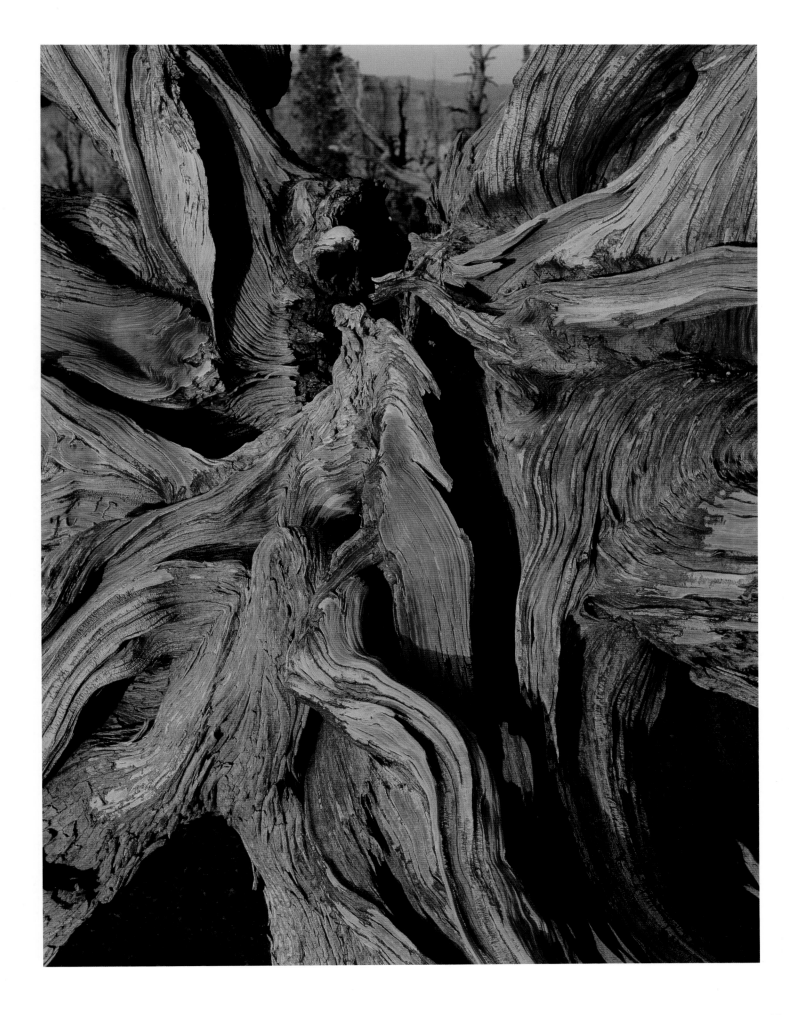

Near Yovimpa Point, the limits of life's endurance are reached. Many bristlecones have died, while others barely embrace life through narrow strips of living bark on the leeward side of the trees. Bryce Canyon's oldest bristlecone pine has survived approximately 1,700 years. High in the White Mountains of California a living bristlecone is 4,600 years old, making the Bryce Canyon tree almost a youngster!

The break of dawn silhouettes scraggly forms of bristlecone pines southeast of Bryce Point. Despite their longevity, the bristlecones of Bryce Canyon seldom grow taller than 25 feet.

The cone of a bristlecone pine holds the opportunity to sow
a seedling whose time on earth may span a millennium.
During its life the bristlecone may witness more than half a
million sunrises, yet reproduce itself only once—if it is lucky.

Two weathered cones from a bristlecone pine rest among
greenleaf manzanita deadwood on the crest of The
Promontory. Decomposition returns scant nutrients to the
limestone gravel soil.

The full moon rises over a small grove of bristlecone pines. Every adaptation of these amazing trees seems geared toward long life. The foxtail-like branches retain bundles of needles for 25 to 30 years.

Ponderosa pine needles rest on a gravel ridge where the wind has swept away most of the snow. Unlike bristlecone pines, ponderosa pine needles turn brown and fall after three to five years.

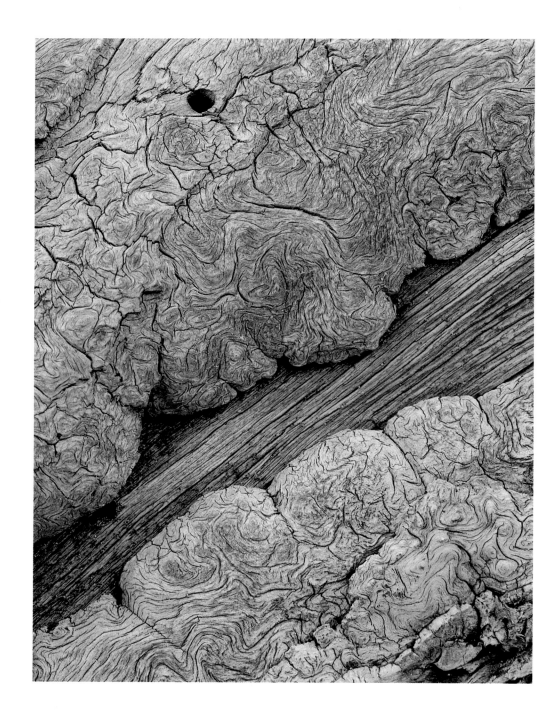

Perhaps lightning produced the scar that was partially healed by intricately grained sapwood. Eventually, this ponderosa pine succumbed to the elements. The pattern of its wood, silvered by decades of exposure, enhances the magical scenery below Bryce Point.

A quaking aspen near Sunset Point produces a riot of autumn color that surpasses the brilliant orange, red, and pink of the Claron Limestone. Soon the aspen will be bare, and Bryce Canyon will fall into the grip of winter.

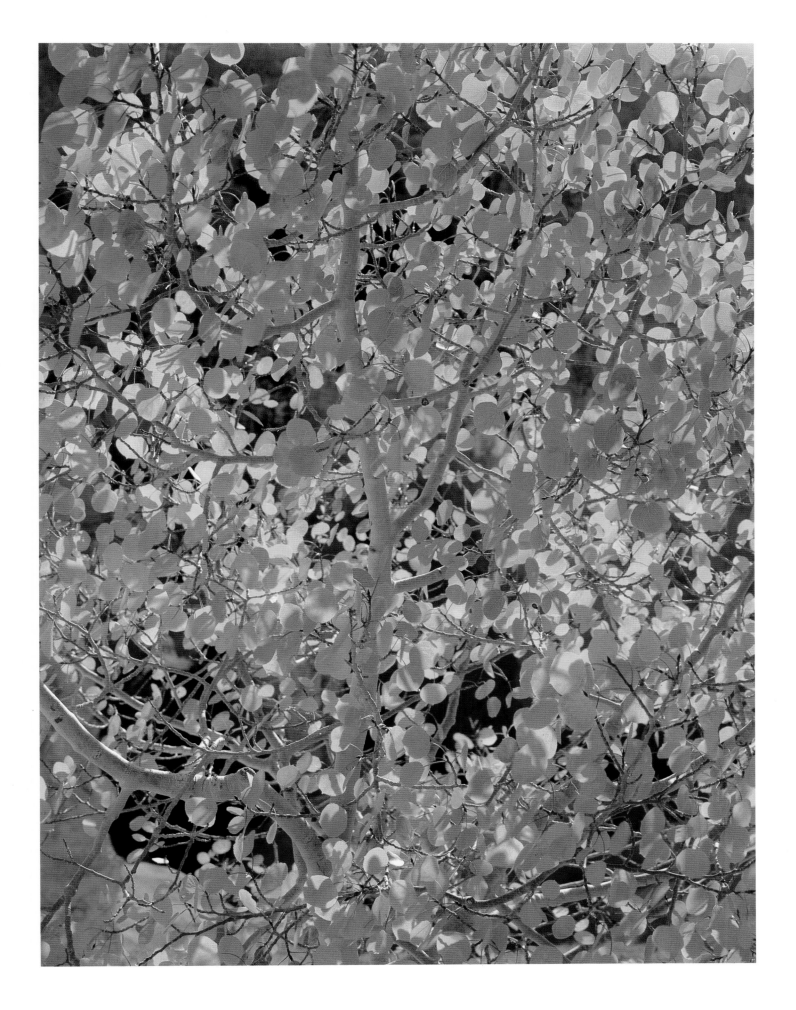

Upturned needles of a white fir capture quaking aspen leaves
near Natural Bridge. Aspens pioneer open spaces and
eventually are overgrown by climax forests of spruce and fir.

Golden color of quaking aspen near Yovimpa Pass conveys
the warmth of a summer gone. Autumn colors usually reach
their peak during the last two weeks of September on Utah's
high plateaus.

A creek in Jolley Hollow reflects the golden color of
surrounding canyon walls. Water derived from springs is clear
and cold. The torrents following summer thunderstorms
transport slurries of grayish-pink mud and debris.

Leaves of water birch rest on cobbles of Claron Limestone
in Jolley Hollow. As their name implies, water birches grow
in canyon country where their roots tap a year-around source
of moisture.

Lichens decorate a Claron Limestone boulder in Jolley Hollow. These pioneering organisms that help decompose rock into soil represent a cooperative living arrangement between fungi and algae.

A colorful understory of bigtooth maple flourishes along Lower Podunk Creek. Vibrant colors of bigtooth maple rival the most brilliant hues found in sugar maples and red maples of the eastern states.

Trees weakened by lightning strikes, old age, infections of
dwarf mistletoe, or drought are likely targets for bark beetles.
Bark peeling off this recently killed ponderosa pine produces
a colorful and interesting pattern.

A depression in the east slope of The Promontory captures
ponderosa pine cones, branches, and rocks as they roll
downhill. Exposure has weathered the scene to a
distinguished shade of silver-gray.

Clouds of a late-winter storm gather behind Natural Bridge. This arch, produced in part by chemical weathering of the Claron Formation, is 54 feet wide.

Following a night of subzero temperatures, back-lit frost illuminates Douglas fir and ponderosa pines on the Paunsaugunt Plateau. The coldest temperature recorded at Bryce Canyon was a frigid −29°F.

Lenticular clouds fill the sky above the Paria Amphitheater in this view of the Sinking Ship and Table Cliff Plateau from the Queen's Garden Trail. Winter is a time of exquisite beauty at Bryce Canyon.

Brilliant snow accents Claron Formation hoodoos in Fairyland Canyon. To the right of the Sinking Ship, the volcanic cone of Navajo Mountain, 82 miles away, looms on the horizon. The clear air of winter offers superb visibility.

The efforts of breaking trail via snowshoes or crosscountry skis are richly rewarded by views of Bryce Canyon's stupendous winter scenery. An unnamed "castle" looms over the Peekaboo Trail.

Along the Fairyland Loop Trail in Campbell Canyon, a lone spire rises above a snowy hill.

Overleaf: Fresh snow blankets hundreds of hoodoos comprising The Silent City.

Erosion working inward from both sides of a narrow wall
sculpted arches in The Wall of Windows. Even on frigid
winter days, ridges and walls facing the sun experience
melting of their surface snow. Water seeping into cracks then
freezes at night. The resulting expansion opens cracks and
speeds the erosive process.

One feels small when lying on one's back and peering straight
up at two towering Douglas firs within the narrow confines of
Wall Street. Snow resting on ledges imparts to the canyon
walls an appearance of a layer cake with white icing.

Heavy snow drapes spruce and fir beneath the rim in the southern portion of Bryce Canyon. A light fog lends an ethereal mood to the peaceful scene.

At Paria View, the Pink Cliffs drop nearly 700 feet to the floor of a beautiful valley embracing Yellow Creek. Toward the southeastern horizon, late afternoon sunlight highlights the edge of the White Cliffs.

Hoodoo walls more than 600 feet in length and more than 200 feet high flank narrow passageways of The Silent City. The most extensive set of primary wall hoodoos in the park occurs between Sunset Point and Inspiration Point.

Fresh snow blankets the Bryce Amphitheater viewed from below Sunrise Point. Freeze-and-thaw cycles occur as many as 200 days a year beneath the rim, hastening erosion.

Severe winds often accompany winter storms that dump up to 25 inches of snow upon Bryce Canyon. Wind-sculpted drifts decorate the edge of the Paunsaugunt Plateau near Upper Inspiration Point.

Snow-capped boughs of a ponderosa pine frame a hoodoo with the likeness of Queen Victoria in the Queen's Garden. Most of the park's erosional forms remain unnamed.

Rime ice coats a ponderosa pine as winter fog envelops the Bryce Canyon rim. The high elevation of the Paunsaugunt Plateau often causes Bryce Canyon to be in the clouds.

Morning frost accents icicles hanging from the boughs of a ponderosa pine. Tiny ice crystals wafted by a gentle wind glimmer in the sun.

Overleaf: A few ponderosa and bristlecone pines grow on the badlands west of Bristlecone Point.

Ice stalactites and stalagmites decorate Mossy Cave when the air remains well below freezing. The 41°F temperature of spring water seeping from the roof equals Bryce Canyon's mean annual temperature.

Snow, hoar frost, and icicles cling to vegetation lining the runoff stream departing Mossy Cave. Surface water quickly disappears beneath thick alluvium clogging the stream bed.

Frost glistens on a Rocky Mountain juniper on a below-zero morning at Bryce Canyon.

Cedar Breaks

Cedar Breaks National Monument, 38 miles west of Bryce Canyon as the raven flies, forms part of the western rim of the 10,500-foot Markagunt Plateau. The badlands and hoodoos of Cedar Breaks look similar to Bryce Canyon and erode from the same colorful Claron Formation. Dusk from Sunset View is a quiet time at Cedar Breaks.

Behind the rim of Cedar Breaks dwells a dark forest of
spruce, fir, and bristlecone pine. Fendler meadowrue imparts
a splash of yellow among the boughs of a Douglas fir.

An ancient bristlecone pine has overlooked Cedar Breaks
from Spectra Point for the past 1,600 years. Nurtured by an
average of 30 inches of annual precipitation, the bristlecones
of Cedar Breaks generally grow larger, though not necessarily
older, than those at Bryce Canyon.

The elevation drops more than 2,300 feet from Chessman
Ridge at the edge of the Markagunt Plateau to where
Ashdown Creek departs the monument two miles to the
west. The badland-and-hoodoo-forming Claron deposits of
Cedar Breaks are almost 2½ times thicker than the same
deposits at Bryce Canyon.

Kodachrome Basin

Southeast of Cannonville in the Paria Valley below Bryce Canyon is an exquisite little state park. Kodachrome Basin was named in 1949 by an expedition of the National Geographic Society. The rich reds, oranges, browns, and greys of the oddly shaped Entrada, Henrieville, and Tropic-Dakota Formations could for the first time be faithfully recorded on Kodachrome film introduced by Eastman Kodak in 1935.

At an elevation of 6,000 feet, Kodachrome Basin sits squarely in the Utah juniper and pinyon pine forest. A conglomerate pipe rising behind the red dome of Entrada Sandstone may have resulted from earthquake activity along the Paunsaugunt Fault settling rock and forcing a slurry of water and gravel upward through deposits of sand. The pipe solidified into rock, and the soft sandstone eroded away.

Red Canyon

Most visitors to Bryce Canyon get their first look at the region's colorful hoodoos while driving through Red Canyon, part of Dixie National Forest. Iron oxides color the formations brilliant red.

Half of Bryce Canyon National Park comprises the beautiful landscape of odd erosional forms and weather-sculpted trees. The other half of the park is the view looking straight up. Bryce Canyon is blessed with excellent air quality and minimal nighttime light pollution. The Milky Way viewed from Sunrise Point at midnight glistens like a thousand jewels in the incredibly clear air.